THE BLIND EYE

by the same author

poetry
NIL NIL
GOD'S GIFT TO WOMEN
THE EYES (a version of *Antonio Machado*)
LANDING LIGHT
ORPHEUS (a version of Rilke's *Die Sonette an Orpheus*)

aphorism
THE BOOK OF SHADOWS

as editor
101 SONNETS
ROBERT BURNS: SELECTED POEMS
LAST WORDS (with Jo Shapcott)
DON'T ASK ME WHAT I MEAN (with Clare Brown)
NEW BRITISH POETS (with Charles Simic)

The Blind Eye

A BOOK OF LATE ADVICE

Don Paterson

faber and faber

First published in 2007
by Faber and Faber Limited
3 Queen Square London WC1N 3AU

Typeset in Minion by Faber and Faber Limited
Printed in England by Mackays of Chatham plc

A CIP record for this book
is available from the British Library

ISBN 978-0-571-23382-3

10 9 8 7 6 5 4 3 2 1

for David

THE BLIND SIDE

THE BLIND EYE

As a native Damascene, all my revelations came on the road to elsewhere. All were eclipses, all were skies falling silent.

§

The male genitals are worn externally as evolution is in the process of expelling them from the body. Another million years and they'll be stored in a drawer.

§

I can see exactly what *not* to do at the moment. No doubt through the usual process of elimination I'll arrive at my favourite strategy of total paralysis.

§

Ego-surfing again, four months since I last dared: the hit-count tripled, nearly all of them namechecks by brand-new enemies, or recruits to the army of doppelgängers – champion disco-dancers, Alaskan Romanticists, men who teach juggling, fuck donkeys, or put miniature combine harvesters in bottles . . . Of whom I would have known nothing, if vanity hadn't tricked me into putting my head round this mirrored corridor of hell again. Good that at least one of our sins now carries its immediate terrestrial punishment.

§

Everything is driven towards entropy, and yet everywhere aspires to the order still inscribed in it by our primal singularity, our cosmic egg – and falls into sphere, orbit, season and pulse. But how sad to find yourself born into a universe founded on the principle of *nostalgia*.

§

With your back to the wall, always pay a compliment. Even your mugger or torturer is not immune to flattery, and still capable of being a little disarmed by a word of congratulation on their choice of footwear or superior technique.

§

I wonder if anyone was ever tempted to play a trick on Helen Keller, and communicate to her that she was really dead. Then again, I once played the same trick on myself, and have done nothing but seek a minute-by-minute reassurance from everything since. So this, dear, is why I touch everyone all the time; I truly wish it *was* something as discriminating as lasciviousness. You will see me display the same overfamiliarity towards the furniture.

§

Whale to the ocean, bird to the sky, man to his dream.

§

In hell, the Postmoderns are awarded a huge, sensitive and critically informed general readership. I wish them sales; I wish them the *book group* . . .

§

No sense steps into the same word twice.

§

The Calvinist knife-edge. Self-loathing gets me out of bed in the morning; but for years it kept me in it.

§

The aphorism: too much too soon or too little too late, but never just enough for the time being.

§

After a reading in Rotterdam, a woman came up to me and complimented me on my performance. I half-heard her, and made her repeat what she had just said. 'Sorry!' I replied, 'I just wanted to hear you say it twice . . .' My weak little joke was either lost on her, or somehow fatally misjudged; she threw up her hands in despair and stormed off. *I can now turn on a sixpence*, I thought to myself, *compress the effect of several years of my acquaintance into a matter of seconds . . .*

§

Poetry! What a fine thing to be working in a medium that brings out the best only in the murderous soul of the poet, and quite the very worst in everyone else. Even a limerick will dig out the one grain of ugly ambition in the heart of a saint.

§

An afternoon watching the Paralympics, the 100 m Butter-
fly won by a swimmer with no arms, head-butting the end
of the pool in order to finish. An astonishing performance,
though to my great shame I found myself wishing that the
human spirit would sometimes triumph just a little *less*.

§

When I was ill, I could hear the rhythmic ictus in all conversation, as clear as a snare-drum; I was as aware of the
speed of the car as if the road were an inch from my own
outstretched fingertips; I saw how my every human
exchange took place without my conscious volition. In
other words: I lost all sense of unreality.

§

Most worrying was his new habit of referring to himself in
the sixth person.

§

I realise whatever slight physical appeal I may once have possessed has long faded, but I should have put more store by it at the time: I foolishly believed I might rely on my personality a little longer.

§

The smartest operators cultivate the very young. Our contemporaries are least able – and least inclined – to guarantee our futures.

§

His song was going so well, until I heard him *express himself* . . . Then I knew I could never play the track again, as I'd spend all my time in anticipatory dread of that one note.

§

His friendship was index-linked to my popularity, and would cool and warm and cool again over the course of a single evening. Immediately after one fortuitous but rather spectacular witticism, he offered me the use of his villa in the Turks and Caicos. Alas, I was fatally emboldened by this small success, and by the time the coffee arrived he had forgotten my name again.

§

Despite taking the Buddha's advice on these matters – 'when you commit a slander, imagine your mouth filled with excrement' – my casual perfidy never fails to astonish me. They will never buy my best defence, which is that it was purely *recreational* . . .

§

In the arts, mere reflection does for epiphany among the poor. A smash-hit piece of local theatre might consist of little more than a public recitation of their street-names and estates. They receive so little self-validation that come Friday night the mere sight of themselves seems revelatory.

§

Sixty years old, and still a paragon of hip insouciance. Still without the courage to fail, even a little.

§

He spent his life paralysed by imaginary protocols.

§

In purgatory, we're shown how narrow were the opportunities we missed; in hell, how narrow were those we took; and in heaven, that nothing could have been otherwise.

§

Sex is better in dreams as the prick has an eye.

§

Okay, *my* memory might be a fiction – but yours is a bloody work-in-progress.

§

High art is simply that which we could never imagine ourselves making, low art that which we *could*. Into the first
we project God, into the second, ourselves; in the first we
seek epiphany, in the second, reflection; the first makes us
feel less low, the second, less alone.

§

Qualification: the human dream isn't a *consensual* reality,
like money, since consensus implies some electoral alternative. An awareness of the dream is merely the realisation
that, while other dreams might exist, we are here obliged
to live under a certain imaginative dictatorship. The material constitution of that wall, that door, we know to be
mostly empty space; but to walk through it would require
our transformation into a shower of neutrinos. Just so, the
veil of the dream may be torn in our meditations; but we
have no choice but to resubscribe to it, *if* we are to wish for
anything but social death. Which is to say that we must
stay lost in the dream to find one another at all.

§

It is not the sophistication but the poverty of a people that is revealed by the local flourishes of their speech. The infinite Sami terms for snow (Eskimos, contrary to popular myth, have need of just two), the eighty shades of green a Nepali can summon by name, are really just the songs of thin economies, which *always* demand this kind of local hyponymic explosion – and are beautiful only to the alien eavesdropper. Scots, for example, has sixty-three words for different kinds of expectoration, being simply our traditional impediment to work. *Kechle*, *kisty-whistle* and *black hoast* may even sound charming to you; to me they do little more than explain the absence of our erotic literature.

§

The poet's only chance of being taken seriously as any kind of thinker depends on the reader also accepting the heresy that there is something in the *style alone* of our presentation, in its pretty sound and its rhetorical flourish, that reveals a little more of the truth than its mere information-content. The Presocratics were all poets; each placed a truth-value on the stylistic virtue of brevity.

§

Please don't be misled by the apparent self-certainty of these utterances; be assured that after each one I nervously delete the words *but that's probably just me, right . . .*

§

After thirty, I came to regard all time spent in the company of men a misuse of a precious and dwindling resource. My notion of decadence was to spend an evening *not* in the company of a woman. I was, however, no decadent, and that was my ruin.

§

As his insults were no different from those I hurl at the mirror every morning, at least my enemy did not have the advantage of surprise. But then I understood: as is so often the case with such unguarded hysterias, he had merely provided a negative litany of his own long-unacknowledged virtues. Among these, it seems we were now required to account his beauty, his originality, his grace, even his fine head of hair. And at the thought of that aging popinjay gurning before *his* mirror each morning . . . I was suddenly mortified with pity.

§

It would be a great help to me personally if they would paint all the planes that are going to crash at some point in their service with a large black stripe. I *abhor* the way I am continually prodded into uninformed decisions.

§

I sometimes wonder if my meditations have won me anything more than *estrangement*, the right to wake up every morning as a bald white monkey with gravity issues.

§

My poor *Socialist Worker* friend . . . He confessed to me that he had just spent £180 on a new donkey-jacket, which is now only available as an item of *couture* . . .

§

The emotional monotony of high Modernism. An anec-
dotal proof: look at how in *Amadeus* Peter Shaffer used
Mozart's own music to illustrate every episode in the com-
poser's life: his grief, joy, angst, love, his pranks, frustration, hilarity . . . Now: imagine a life of Schoenberg,
similarly scored. In every scene – tennis court, birthday
party, love-, birth- or death-bed – you'd be expecting an
escaped lunatic in a fright mask to burst from the cup-
board with an axe.

§

No one has ever adequately explained to me the self-
evident merit in sensitivity. I spent my first seventeen years
feeling everything, and the only place it got me was the
mental ward. There is also something base about art which
provokes us merely to *suffer* more than we need to, and in
doing so blunting our more sophisticated responses.

§

That night we saw through him, all of us, and he knew it. O it was a terrible thing to then watch a man try to *substantialise* himself.

§

It appeared clear from his letters and emails that this saintly individual was a petty and embittered monster. Then it later emerged, from the testimony of his close friends, that he was nothing of the sort, and capable of many discreet and time-consuming acts of charity. But then it further emerged, from the testimony of his abused wife and damaged children, to what extent his friends were mistaken. And then one day they found his secret journal, where his own inner torment – as well as his early brutalisation at the hands of his father – was revealed, after which it was hard not to forgive him everything . . . Our error lay in our sentimental desire to read him as a recursive series, with each nested personality revealing a deeper truth. He was merely, like everyone else, a complete *mess*; an answer we are never satisfied with.

§

The brain is a tool for conjuring meaning from the void; and since the void is also *literally* our mother and father, it is a literal measure, if not of the void's own desire for meaning, then at least of its parental ambition for us.

§

What kills the writer, in the end, is the absence of a direct causal relationship between effort and reward. Thus it is rarely true *work*, in any way our bodies can understand. A free day, all the kids off to their grandmother's, the house deathly quiet; half an hour's meditation; a cafetière of Costa Rica in the study; no sound but the rain dripping from the trees in the back garden through the open window . . . And I cannot introduce two words to one another without them falling out immediately. Today, feeling exhausted, ill, over-weight, the house full of yelling, my mind a roiling broth of fear and resentment and professional jealousy – a dozen problems I have pored over for weeks have been solved in twenty minutes flat. I end the day feeling worse than ever, as if I had accomplished nothing at all.

§

They awoke in a dark and windowless room, and all had forgotten how long they had slept. After a month of blindness they found a torch, which some declared an abomination, and retreated to the shadows forever. Then those with a torch found a watch, which read twelve; and some decided it was midnight, and some noon, and thereafter both parties developed their separate cultures.

§

Remove the error of self, and being here once is the identically equivalent miracle (if you can now conscionably use such a word) to being here again. The life now is already life after death, as remarkably so as any you might live in the future. Nothing will constitute the new you except the organism whose evolution has demanded, just as yours does now, the construction of another phantom centre. So while the next thing 'we' will indisputably know is another reawakening, the clever self-creation of the brief soul of something or other, we might as well face up to the fact that – our infinite vegetable slumberings notwithstanding – we'll do well to make a rat or jellyfish; more likely some bizarre phenotype a few million light-years distant. The best we can pray for is that there is a secret economy at work, whereby a presently inscrutable, quantum-tunnelled aspect of our human schooling is converted to some universal currency and smuggled over. If I'm brutally honest, though, I can assemble little evidence to offer myself that I 'got lucky' this time round, and that the experience is worth repeating. What I think of as a fondness for being human is really just an attachment to being me, that is – to nothing at all.

§

No, I'm not obsessed with myself, just *the* self; I could be just as easily mesmerised by yours, if it were as readily available for study.

§

When her reputation was at its height a quarter-century ago, ah . . . ne'er had public opinion so well anticipated the judgement of posterity; she was *sui generis*, and dedicated her career to an elaborate proof of this fact, by elimination: not only was every writer wholly in the debt of some other, but her main aesthetic premise was that *all the things of the world* were in themselves mere realia, repro, helpless imitators of one another. Now her star had faded, she was obsessed with plagiarism, and saw it everywhere: it was the only way she could insist we were all still paying her homage.

§

Email allows me to indulge my new meditative technique: annihilation via impersonation. I answer each letter in my interlocutor's voice, and forty responses later I am no one and everyone.

§

The truer we sing, the more we violate our own boundaries, and the more our bodies protest; those who sing truest are all suicides.

§

My deeper ignorances I intend to cure by reincarnation. Not without its own inconveniences, to be sure, but fewer than the prospect of actual *study*.

§

The strongest illusions loom so close we are blind to them, since they are continuous with our thought, and invisibly guide its content and direction. The original thinkers find the thumbnail purchase between the surface of their ideas and those distorting lenses, and then prise open the space in which they can look at them, not through them. Not without its dangers, as incompetence can mean self-operation on the *real* mind, which always leaves it damaged. (I think of my friend, now resigned to wearing glasses for life: waking drunk in the small hours, he was convinced he had forgotten to take out his contact lenses, and spent half an hour trying to remove his own corneas.) Alas they so often emerge as the only means by which the dream can be brought into focus, and so must be sadly replaced in their original position.

§

I wake up crapulous and half-suicidal in a hotel room at 5.45 a.m., exhausted by my sweats and nightmares. I grope for the remote, and the breakfast show. A radiant woman is being interviewed, and the caption below her simply reads *Former Sufferer* . . .

§

The litany of my old lovers, my beautiful Linnaean taxonomy, my floral tribute.

§

I gave up origami at twelve because anything I created was closer to Neal Elias, the folder I liked least, than to a divine like Ligia Montoya or Yoshizawa. I have met many musicians with the same problem: one bassist spent his life practising to sound like Charles Mingus and ended up a double for the facile technomaniac Niels-Henning Ørsted Pedersen. But Mingus didn't practise to be Mingus; he sounded like Mingus after six months on the instrument. What made him Mingus was *not imitable*; it lay in a singular spirit, physiology and psychopathology. What *is* most imitable in a style, while perhaps the most superficially characteristic, usually emerges as the least enviable thing about it.

§

Only the best poets can risk simplicity. The rest of us are merely exposed by it. Only those same poets can risk complexity too: the rest invariably fail to realise the greatly increased responsibility towards *clarity* that it demands. Nonetheless so many rush towards it, knowing their faults are here best concealed.

§

The Greeks right again. The light indeed pours from our eyes – its little, dim, narrow human light: we stand before the world like a projectionist behind his dusty cone of shadows, illuminating only what we already know.

§

Certain events, if repeated often enough, allow their internal eidolon to be conjured at will. The fingertips on the fretboard, the slalom of the tongue on her thigh, the weight of the book, the screw on the south-westernmost quadrant of the cue-ball . . . All these things access my realm of waking dream.

§

We were strolling along the street, and passed a couple of sleepy undergraduates. Suddenly my companion interjected – *so then I shot him in the face – terrible fucking mess, brains all up the walls* . . . for no reason other than to bring a little colour into the lives of his eavesdroppers. He then resumed our conversation on Sondheim.

§

In this life, only *older* holds out the genuine possibility of our not being us.

§

In its final convulsions, the imperial nation follows exactly the psychotic narrative: losing all sense of itself, it concentrates its energies at the rim, hollows itself out from the centre, and then implodes, all the while screaming that it is Jesus Christ.

§

The most disturbing thing about children learning to speak is discovering what homicidal whims have been preoccupying the two-year-old mind.

§

Yet again, I find a basic grammatical error in a quoted passage of mine. Always the same damn thing – a disagreement of number or mood or person, and always for the same reason: I cannot attend to the start of a long sentence carefully enough to retain its subject in my mind, and finish it under the impression I have been working with an entirely different one. All the evidence I need that I have no talent at all for even the most narrow overview, like those autistics for whom the world is all detail and no pattern. I imagine all similarly afflicted individuals develop the same obsession with Unity, as their Brigadoon, their romantic impossible elsewhere.

§

In our experience of the natural sublime, nothing is transcended except the human dream, as we are translated briefly into a state of simple animal belonging. Our revelation on these occasions is precisely *not* the Great Presence, but its summary disappearance – leaving us a happily earthbound monkey, suddenly and joyously continuous with their element. When God *really* dies – along with all his subtle and pervasive ghosts, his stubbornly loyal, reluctantly disbanding retinue – we're back home again. We have been utterly betrayed by those fancy intercessors of ours, who led us only into dismal exile.

§

When you respond by acting just as they do, low men immediately impute to you their own motives, and are torn between fear and camaraderie.

§

Lessons instantly learned, and I pass this on to you urgently: better to forget a woman's birthday altogether than to guess it six months out.

§

The laws of this particular universe favour creatures of a certain size, on planets of a certain gravity, orbiting stars of a certain optimum mass . . . And so on, for twenty other non-negotiable conditions. From which we can quickly extrapolate that the bicycle and the piano are almost certainly *universal solutions*. Nothing makes me more happy or more sad than the thought of my brother or sister sitting, right now, in a room so far distant not even light can pass between us, their rooms furnished with near-identical stuff . . . And dreaming, perhaps, the same cosmic solidarity – that dream, that thought, being the only thing we will ever exchange.

§

The reason for the pillow is that it eliminates the face.

§

Whenever he saw someone reading a Bible, he would spoil it for them by whispering, 'He dies in the end, you know.' I'm always tempted to do the same to anyone I see consulting their diary.

§

L. rather stagily 'insults my integrity', and expects me to be left reeling. I barely understood the offence. He was pulling a face at a blind man.

§

If I existed before this life and yet can recall nothing of it, then there is no 'I' that can be sensibly discussed beyond its present manifestation. Yet I have no doubt that I *have* existed before, simply because to say otherwise is to commit the Ptolemaic error of declaring one's present situation unique and miraculous. In this life my true family is a set with only one member; the minds of the others can be read but never penetrated. Nor can any fraternity be extended to the chain of my previous 'I's; all the links are uncoupled, and there is no lineage to pursue. Therefore my lives prior to this incarnation must encompass all the things that have ever been. Having no allegiance to any single mind, I discover myself nowhere and everywhere. My mind was there dispersed, and for fourteen billion years I partook of *all* lives, as the as-yet-uncondensed minds beyond my death now partake of my own. This leaves my present mind as a mere designated point, an inspissation of a universal mind that has condensed in me for no reason but the one it now chooses for itself: to uncover its own nature. I thought this a romantic fallacy, right up to the sudden and horrified registration of its demonstrable truth: we are matter; thinking is what we *do*

here; therefore we are not the slaves but the primary agents
of that universal mind. I have *sole responsibility*.

§

You've made a *blog* . . . Clever boy! Next: flushing.

§

Naturally, he had not once contemplated the possibility
that the subject of his life's study might have been an idiot.
His meticulous exegeses of the poems of X were about as
edifying as the spectacle of a great scientist performing the
microscopic dissection of a hamburger.

§

She insisted on absolute honesty, so I told her everything. I never saw her again, but at least I had spared the next guy the same ordeal.

§

Unthinkable that I would ever put my own happiness – whatever the hell *that* is – before anyone else's. Alas when all the people whose happiness I had put first realised the extent of their company, they were considerably less moved by my selflessness.

§

A beautiful man or woman I do not know steps with me into an empty lift, still ripe with the bad fart of the previous occupant – and I experience an immediate, specific, visceral revulsion towards *them*. The immaculate are tainted waiting to happen.

§

That land, the extralinguistic wilderness, has a different overseer; our nervous references, our little letters of introduction from the small gods of tongue and word, are all without value there. So we really only have three choices: to return empty-handed, and face the shame; to fake both the journey and the goods; or to steal the poem. Hence the flu symptoms and sheer terror that often accompany our conduction of the most trivial lyric.

§

He could contrive, he knew, even an inauthentic suicide; his merely staying alive was his one concession to good taste.

§

I had never had such a thing before: a *declared* enemy. But I'd be lost without him now. It's a feeling so close to love. I *made* him, as one makes a poem or a child, by accident *and* design.

§

If we look hard enough, we can always find both insight and beauty in meaningless verse; though we are paying no compliment whatsoever to the *poem*, but only to our own intelligence – in whose company we have merely spent a little uninterrupted time.

§

Critics all have this idea that authors inhabit another dimensional realm, right up to their first smack in the mouth – which feels to them quite miraculous, being their sex-dream come true.

§

What I find most offensive is the world's presumption that it has *rescued* me from non-existence, its . . . pleased expression.

§

I was always pretty good at low-grade luck, those sad little
two-cherry windfalls, and could always whistle up the yel-
low roof-light of the empty cab at three in the morning,
the half-wish of the faint meteor, that wee treasurable fris-
son of the envelope icon on the mobile . . . But my psychic
aim is catastrophic. There are days when I can make the
phone ring at will, but it's always the last person I want to
hear from. If you want some roses delivered out the blue
from a secret admirer, I can probably arrange it for you, if
you don't mind them being from your psychopathic driving instructor.

§

Nightmare: that consciousness might never take another
form but this phantom centre, whose presence in others
we can only confirm by indirect means. I have felt myself
on the verge of tearing lovers limb from limb, to find that
heart I had dreamt of being lost within . . . Were it all to be
definitively proven – were we to know ourselves locked
into the individual soul *forever* – the whole human project
would fold its hand tomorrow.

§

He could not wash her away; his hands would smell of her sex for days afterwards. He loved her scent, but her indelibility terrified him, and he knew their meetings were numbered.

§

Faces rarely betray the true feelings of their owners, publicly or privately – with one exception: there is a tiny leakage in all acts of departure. If you attend, with preternatural care, to her eyes in the millisecond just prior to your turning your back to leave the room . . . There you will learn the very worst of what she thinks of you.

§

From the cloud to the zip-fastener, the silver birch to the dirty bomb, everything *arose* – and so must be considered a member of the set of natural objects.

§

The trouble with the blind eye is that it looks identical to
the seeing kind; and waving a hand in front of it ruins
everything, either way.

§

Boredom, in its uncut state, is a *force*. To know it takes a
mind of unassuagable restlessness – which pays that mind
no compliment, as it implies neither curiosity nor any particular capacity for insight. Nor can such a mind ever dis-
arm its own boredom by meditating upon nothing.
Instead it perfects its obsession, its meditation upon *one*
thing: in this we also lose the self, but bargain away the
whole world too, in exchange for a profound intimacy
with the Speyside malts, postage stamps, death, the feet of
women.

§

When you first make love to the beloved, you enter a zone of unfocus as your face approaches hers . . . From which she reappears, in close-up, as a stranger. With anyone *but* the beloved, the experience is smoothly gradated; but such is the beloved's conflation with our *angel*, we know they have fallen to be with us, changed their essential nature for the sake of human love . . . And there our gratitude is bound to be mixed. Indeed, at first sight, she can look heartbreakingly close to the most terrifying thing you have ever seen.

§

Wouldn't it be wonderful if our children's religious education began and ended with the single sentence: *Kids – I'm afraid no one has the first clue why we're here.*

§

He was no fool, and yet he had written a book by a fool. As a dramatic monologue it would have been a triumph of sustained impersonation, had we not suspected that *fool* was the beginning and end of his literary repertoire.

§

Your manifest uncertainty is the best guarantor of the truth of your statement, not your wise voice.

§

Read a whole book of aphorisms by N. It felt like swallowing an entire bottle of a homeopathic remedy, whose total absence of effect did nothing but reinforce my suspicion that the aphorism is only useful in small measured doses – but even then it's only a kind of intellectual placebo, prompting ideas the reader should have prompted in themselves anyway.

§

He liked to think of himself as a thorn in our side; but he was a much smaller man than he imagined himself, and merely a pain in the arse.

§

All sustained atonality is perceived by the human ear (which, being a thing of nature, has *grown* around the tonic) as unresolved dominant harmony. As symbolic substitutes for dominant and tonic resolution, we have dissonance and assuaging silence. If the dissonance lasts for several minutes, nervous anticipation and prayers for *peace* give way to a resignation to a state of hopeless irresolution; several hours of it induce a psychotic state equivalent to a month of front-line warfare. After surviving *Moses und Aron* I emerged perfectly calm, and ready to kill a man with my bare hands.

§

Doors, those merciful *conceits*, those blind eyes of the house . . . As if your daughter or brother or friend wasn't beating off or taking a shit six feet from where you stood.

§

By the age of eleven, I was finally exasperated with my parents. I knew I had been left with no alternative but to fuck *myself* up.

§

He *made* K. review his book; K. then laboured day and night until he found a form of words so exquisitely fitted to its every stylistic deformity, slouch and love-handle that it would never shrug it off again.

§

A medium once told me that in my previous incarnation I had been a bluebottle who had caused an accident in a private plane, in which an evil man had been killed. As a result of that inadvertent heroism I had been karmically fast-tracked, despite the opposition of several high-ranking devas. I was immediately convinced of the truth of this story, and it continues to explain everything.

§

Allowed myself a smile this morning at a letter innocently referring to 'my love of the aphoristic form'. Christ – do you think if I really had a *choice*, I would write *this*? We occupy the margins through fate, not allegiance.

§

M. threw everything P. wrote back in his face. So P. scribbled twenty lines of garbage, and told M. it was a translation of a fragment found in Desnos' journal, dated the month he was arrested by the Gestapo. M. found it perfectly marvellous. Anyone who can dismiss you *comprehensively* merely despises you on principle, but these same individuals venerate on principle too; no disinterested judgement will ever distort their immaculate prejudice.

§

The fuel-injected articulacy of everything we write in infatuation or anger. Latin for the fury, love's Anglo-Saxon tropes . . . No wonder writers wreck their lives trying to maintain these two states.

§

I have owed a slight acquaintance, K., an email for six months. This morning I hear that he has died. My single obsequy was to cross him off my to-do list, and feel my burden lighten a little. I even caught myself wondering if there might be something in this that could be worked up into a general strategy.

§

Of all the layers of dream that govern this life, the deepest and most catastrophic is that of our solitariness; only death cures it, and even then only by cessation, not awakening.

§

One reason so many women fell in love with him was that he was given, mid-sentence and with no warning, to find himself suddenly overwhelmed by a kind of infinitely distracted silence . . . For a few seconds, possessed by something so far beyond the earth, no one could reasonably be jealous of it; so they drew upon their unreasonable jealousy to fuel their own . . . alternative diversions. It was many years before it was diagnosed as petit mal seizure.

§

We are all the thinking that matter does round here; but to acknowledge as much for one second would kill us out-right. We are children, and not yet ready for that kind of responsibility. Hence our delegation of the whole business to our heavenly fathers and mothers.

§

'Now I'll read a *funny* poem.' *Oh*, I thought. *I'll be the judge of* that.

§

'Now I'll read a long poem.' It was then I finally admitted to myself that the poetry reading was *no night out*.

§

The more obscure the activity, the more certain the opinion of its critics. Who would have suspected, for example, that the aphorism had so many *exact* definitions . . .

§

The self is a universal vanishing point.

§

'When I die,' he told me, 'I want every organ in my body to be completely *fucked*.' And so it was: they found his twenty-stone carcass on the sofa, soaked in spilt beer and melted Häagen-Dazs, smiling like the Buddha, and not a cell of him worth donating. As ambitions go, by no means the worst: to have exhausted the organism, to have wasted *nothing* . . .

§

The global market means that money can be finally free of any *sentimental* attachment to place – meaning that an entire workforce might find itself instantaneously relocated to a more labour-law- and tax-friendly locale, since their changes of name and physical organism are now mere details. Furthermore, by definition no one can pull out of a universal game: which is to say no single country or city can withdraw to devote its own resources to, say, narrowing the gap between its working class and its bourgeoisie to an inoffensive distance without its appearing self-radicalised. If the only permissible independent economies are transnational corporations, no country or city on earth can be free from the threat of their sudden disinvestment or disfavour, their sequestration of natural resources, or their corruption of local officials. Thus whole nations are required to resign themselves to permanent and intolerable inequalities. Utter hopelessness does not give rise to small hopes, however, but great ones: ideology and ideologue soon follow. Of course wherever they arise, liberal reform has not a hope in hell. Bad enough, but far worse, globalisation did not notice the shadow it dragged behind it in the late day. The ideologies have *themselves* gone global, and can now recruit in every dark nook in the planet where the gap sufficiently outrages, where young men and women sit up late filming their goodbyes and instructions for their exequies. Their annihilation of tribal rivals and bus-loads of civilians are mere range-finding; their weapon is new. Disney, Time Warner, Wal-Mart, General Electric, Halliburton, Exxon: welcome to your flexible workforce.

§

I could not rouse myself from the nightmare; mercifully I was not alone in bed, and she heard my muffled cries and liberated me. The dream, I told her, was simply that I had no body to wake to, and hence no way out of the dream. Yet now that I was awake, it was no better. I knew I was still dreaming bodiless, and that not even death itself could spring me from it, and that all my life had been a mere diversion from this rising panic.

§

There *is* a universal eye, but it sees only through our own: our every blink blinds it.

§

Here is a very bad aphorism for the purpose of illustrative quotation.

§

I asked her what she thought had given our relationship its longevity, and so initiated – I quickly realised – the first discussion of our relationship we had ever had. We were finished in a month.

§

Ah, that whey-faced lank-haired lad, all his ideas, exquisitely, just a little beyond his means . . . He was, I believe, the author of a little book about the ringtone phenomenon; the mere intonation of his name seems, even now, to fill the room with the smell of stale semen and the clicking of Game Boys. Okay . . . did I mention that his review of my poetry was so bad even *I* could not accept it? I was grateful, nonetheless, that he allowed me to establish the very worst I could think of myself.

§

My worst sins I committed in pursuit of forgiveness for lesser. I can understand the ultimate balm of genocide: the elimination of guilt through the annihilation of all possible forgivers.

§

A day lost in failed spells, trying to conjure a ring from the phone: all those miserable countdowns to nothing, to zero, to no event.

§

Despite their not sharing a single physical or temperamental characteristic, Y became convinced he was the model for the protagonist in X's novel, and read the whole book as a litany of well-aimed, excoriating insult. His friends were worried for him, knew he was being paranoid and egotistical, and did their best to assure him of his error. X, meanwhile, shrugged and watched Y tear himself apart, knowing he had done his work beautifully.

§

Only someone with the *genuine* arrogance of a Rimbaud
or a Cantona could declare their retirement and actually
mean it. To make a single return to the stage is to reveal
oneself a mere applause-monkey.

§

No, you confuse having entertained my idea with having
merely *read* it; hence the ease of your dismissal.

§

I was so practised in disappointment, I absorbed the blow
of her leaving me almost effortlessly. Allowing yourself to
be *constructed* by the lover means you have been a different
man from the start; I merely left his body behind like a
husk, and let him take the punch. (I watched him double
up, as from above.) The loveless wraith of me was then
free to wander, looking for my new instructions.

§

I did not reciprocate her love until I realised the value
other men had placed on her; and then who could *not*?
Can any man honestly say that he accounts his worth in
his own private and unique currency?

§

We always made love with our eyes closed; open, they were
coupled by a fibre-optic cable, streaming intolerable tera-
bytes of data.

§

The lapidary coldness of the aphorism assuages a grief or a
grievance far better than the poem. It erects a stone over
each individual hurt.

§

My plan was to involve her in an act of such intimacy as to both repel and enslave her: I had long understood the power of our disgusted complicities. But *nothing* could enslave her, *nothing* could repel her; and in reaching my own extremes I realised the game had been hers all along, and that I had lost my mind months ago.

§

Fate's book, but my italics.

§

Her so suddenly quitting in the early stages of our relationship meant I was obliged to hurriedly revise my future; at least this afforded me, I decided, the bravery of a blank canvas I might not otherwise have granted myself. Unfortunately, the new ventures and career-paths I proposed – street-vendor, lunatic, rapist, drunk – seemed oddly in the grip of certain imaginative constraints.

§

If you would win them back: know that the machinery of whatever game you were playing will execute a few extra turns from sheer momentum in the first few days of disconnected silence. Since most people insist on the game ending by its own rules and not its mere discontinuation, your mere refusal to play it (to do nothing, say, when that is *their* prerogative) will bewilder them utterly.

§

Imagining the worst is no talisman against it.

§

If only there was a poetic equivalent of that great sleevenote instruction *play twice before listening* . . .

§

Our love poems are mostly the work of madmen. I laid them at her feet, proudly, as a cat would a half-eaten rat.

§

My friend is an egotist; every blank expression turned towards him he reads as a kind of autism. I am also an egotist: yet every blank expression I read as contempt.

§

He was obsessed with his fallibility, and I cared not a jot for mine. This, together with my gift for instant recantation, put me at a terrifically unfair advantage.

§

My time here has afforded me no enlightenment, though my night-vision has improved enormously. In fact it seems to have evolved as if certain of its future indispensability.

§

With friends and strangers I can be no one; more and more I confine myself to their company. Then one day I enter a room full of acquaintances, and fly into a blind panic: I cannot remember for the life of me who these people think I am . . .

§

He always whispered the bad news in your left ear; always made sure his slanders were printed verso . . . For years he escaped our attention. We knew, vaguely, that evil accompanied him, but thought the two no more connected than the tree and the wind that shook it. Then one day we realised there was no wind: just his own black whistling.

§

Experiments in attachment. My friend has just had his PC wired for broadband. I meet him in the cafe; he looks terrible – his face puffy and pale, his eyes bloodshot . . . He tells me he is now detained, night and day, in downloading every album he ever owned, lost, desired, or was casually intrigued by; he has now stopped even *listening* to them, and spends his time sleeplessly monitoring a progress bar . . . He says *it's like all my birthdays have come at once*, by which I can see he means, precisely, that he feels he is going to *die*.

§

I tried for a while to keep a diary, making one entry at dawn and another on the facing page before I fell asleep. (There are no meridian diaries; anyone able-bodied and under the age of seventy who has the leisure to write one is beneath contempt.) The irreconcilability of the two personalities was so immediately apparent, I quit after a few weeks. The dumb hope of one, then the disillusion of the other – a motif repeated without interruption – depressed me beyond words. I went back to bookending the days, as the human monkey should, with caffeine and alcohol, the newspaper and lovemaking, information and oblivion.

§

Every new poem leaves the last a little exposed, embarrassed, usurped, smacking somehow of *juvenilia* . . .

§

All evening, listening to his wonderful table-talk, I kept finding myself think: *Ah, but in six months you'll be dead, and* I *will have said that . . .*

§

He prided himself on seeing through everyone. Then one evening, at a party, I saw how his focus always fell a little too far ahead of its object; and knew he had entered the realm of phantoms.

§

Silence between lovers always takes a negative or positive charge, and can't be empty or emptied of meaning; though if only one party understands this rule, they are in hell.

§

A fine recording by the seventy-year-old João Gilberto, still singing beautifully at an age when nearly every other singer has gone off . . . But there was nothing in his voice in the first place, no vibrato, no expression, nothing that could ever ripen and rot.

§

I enjoyed L.'s creeping senility. I could have him repeat my favourite stories as often as I wanted, sometimes several times in the space of the same afternoon. X's sudden lurch into his anecdotage, on the other hand, was a disaster: until then, his shyness had prevented our discovering what a *bore* he was.

§

I have the bad habit of deliberately making myself almost worthless in the eyes of those I most admire. This way they will sometimes reveal themselves to me utterly, as they would to a dog . . . Or so I'd like to think: I am unable to credit myself with *anything*, even bringing out the worst in people.

§

Down at the clinic for my in-flight Valium, my usual doctor on holiday. 'How far are you flying?' asks the locum, reckoning the dose. 'Three miles,' I reply, adding inwardly: *you idiot* . . .

§

In the end, the desolate age always turns instinctively to classicism, which if nothing else legislates against certain kinds of disappointment.

§

Language: the category error as belief-system.

§

The rose's night-black is as true as her day-red.

§

It is possible for a woman to say, honestly, that she has thought of her lover all day long – but she will neglect to mention the twenty other things she has kept in her head at the same time. A man ignorant of this ability will be terrified by her declaration, since were it to be his . . . It would amount to a straightforward admission of his own derangement.

§

As we think of the dead, so the immortals think of us: as a fraternity of ghosts, the *ones-who-pass-through* . . .

§

Long conversation with an American academic. I was freely brilliant: I took risks, I made brave and wild connections, I realised *I did not care what he thought of me.* I had fallen into a delicious dream of total immunity, discovering a whole continent that spoke the same language, but yet could do no damage to my name – or at least none I need give a damn about . . .

§

She was married, now – and happy, fat, loquacious, and given to fits of giggling. The metamorphosis had been so sudden, I had the clear sense that the woman in whom I had found such a black mystery had either been just another fantasy of mine, or stuck at some . . . neotenic impasse.

§

Nothing more dangerous than the saviour who mistimes his appearance.

§

Lying still inside her, I was suddenly freed from everything, my term, my fate, like a train that had run off the rails to find itself suddenly moored in the middle of a sunlit field, or a field in darkness.

§

The bleakest and briefest of human literatures, one I have seen men read and be straightaway moved to tears: the price-tag.

§

When I lost my virginity, I flew my *own* sheets from the window, I *myself* bled with relief . . .

§

Eventually most musicians give up listening to their instrument, as I did, and hear only themselves; the real musicians never stop.

§

I still want to come back, one last time, as one of those beautiful charming men. But the line between their desire and the acquisition of its object is drawn so tight, they are vessels of pure karma; they can never depart the earth. To buy into such an individual once would be to buy into him forever.

§

The blush: what evolutionary advantage do we gain in the *publication* of our embarrassment? But then the secret shame rarely had much effect on my future conduct.

§

For a short anthology of pre-emptive strikes, notes on the multiple vanities of the form, etc. – can I please refer you to the afterword of the previous book, where you will find that your cynicism and distaste has not only been fully anticipated but outstripped by the author's own. Even in this accomplishment you will nonetheless find him *taking no pride*.

§

You are physically closer to an acoustic guitar than any other instrument; its body beats and moans through your own, yes, like a lover's. Hence its attraction for losers and loners. The singer-songwriter, of whom Orpheus is the prototype, has his guitar primarily for company, not accompaniment. As he ascended from the dark, it belatedly dawned on Orpheus that he didn't really *need* his girlfriend.

§

I'm always amused by those commentators who nervously insist that the working class's constant use of the word *fuck* is really just 'a form of punctuation'. It is, however, no more or less than what they dread: an inexhaustible river of smelted wrath, a Phlegethon of ancestral grievance . . .

§

The excluded first console themselves by deciding they must form a class of radical, then by perfecting a form of radical behaviour that guarantees that they will never risk the shame of being thrown out again.

§

I had been scrupulous in God's abolition; and nor would I allow the humanist error of allowing his ghost to water-mark my thinking. But then I realised that I had the opportunity to resurrect him by simply *deciding* he existed – and, to my disgust, that there was nothing I desired as much. There was no sophistry in this at all; since the truth was no longer the possession of some inscrutable third party, it no longer existed to be determined, but unilaterally decided. I could construct whatever damn spirit I pleased. I mention this by way of explanation, should you one day find me torn to pieces behind the door of my locked study.

§

'But I don't *think* I could write poetry . . .' Unbelievably, my friend – a successful author in several genres – was serious; she thought there might still be the possibility she *could*, simply because she had never attempted it. Pointless to explain that she would have known from the age of five, or from her parents' stories of her terrifying fevers at that age; that it is *something broken in the head . . .*

§

Dread and rapture are inimical to the composition of poetry, even if the naïf thinks them the ideal states. I'll never write a single decent word at 30,000 feet; if I try, I write black on black, or white on white. The temperament of the act and of the inspiration must somehow be oppositionally ranged, as the ink to the paper.

§

Beware the obsessive between obsessions: if his brain doesn't eat itself, it will eat yours.

§

What have the poets lost now they no longer have their mnemonics? The respect they used to arrogate to themselves through the specific threat: *Would you like me to put something in your head that you can't get out again?*

§

Of course memory is a function of the present – and so is continually subject to revision in the light of what the present reveals. It transpires that she was not the faithful lover you had thought; that when he said those terrible things to you, he had just discovered he was dying . . . Nonetheless we should not concede that we got something badly wrong just because a new perspective alters its sense. All we gain is a *practical* demonstration – for once – that the meaning of our lives is unstable, and its information-content unfixable. All we have is the interpretative act of memory, and its truths are only distinguished from its lies by the sheer luck of their being historically unchallenged. (It is further revealed, let's suppose, that her betrayal was fabricated by a jealous admirer; or that, from his old diaries, it's clear that your behaviour had disgusted him for years . . . and once again, the memories must be sweetened or embittered to taste.) We have no better truth than the present we simply live – one as yet untainted by memory, and so emptied of any meaning.

§

The worst thing about thinking nothing of yourself is that you assume that your behaviour has no consequence. This makes you much more dangerous than the egomaniac, who at least spends all his time calculating for his own effect.

§

Blessed is the wrongdoer who makes no attempt to justify his actions by anything but *pure evil.*

§

Music softens us up for everything; the take-off, the poem, the needle, the bolt.

§

What is it in the middle distance that implies our absence of attention? Short focus signs our concentration; long, our deep or distracted thought. But the eyes of the dead all converge on a point twenty yards away, presumably Death's own range.

§

It may indeed be the case that our new particle accelerators and supercolliders will allow MIT and CERN to verify the membrane-basis of the universe in the next couple of years; this will conclusively prove the universe a monosubstantial unity. Though I have a terrible fear that they will conclusively *fail* . . . Ach, all those televised shamefaced apologies from the Dalai Lama . . .

§

'Trust me, you're *anything* but irresistible –' she said, 'you're just irresist*ing*.' At this she placed her hand on my heart . . . into which it appeared to sink past the wrist. The self expunged in self-disgust is just as absent as any removed by more careful means. Folk can generally go just a little deeper with me than they can with most other people before encountering the resistance of another self. This slight fall they are wont to confuse with intimacy; it's merely the reflection I offer in lieu of a personality of my own.

§

My friend hated book-jackets, and ripped them all off immediately. I think he felt, somehow, that the book was still trying to sell him its contents after he had paid for them. Without its dust-cover, the book is anonymous and valueless. You remove a book-jacket just as you make a lover naked: before their complete possession, they must be removed from the *currency*.

§

There will always be one person who went to their grave knowing Shakespeare only as a moneylender, MacNeice as a poodle-fancier, Feynman as a bongo-player. The great and their little lives.

§

The Middle American is expert in the inflation and amplification of the first person, and *dwells* on it like no one else; as in 'I'm gonna get my fat ol' lazy ass outta here'.

§

Many accounts of torture tend to confirm its vocational aspect; torturers will cheerfully put in a great deal of unpaid overtime. Another reason to accord the vocation no particular respect. The word should be used with a deep neutrality.

§

I would hate that my Christian friend lose his faith. The dreams of the eternal agonies of his close acquaintances were his one source of real pleasure.

§

The underclass rarely use name-contractions, which still require a small excess of love; which is to say more than they have to spare. The children are all called Christopher, Anthony, Margaret, William, Alexandra.

§

The gullible woman is a far scarcer commodity than male fantasies admit. Even for Jesus, the women were all major scalps.

§

There are nice distinctions that will ever remain a mystery to my sex. Today I asked a friend how her affair was progressing. 'It's not an *affair*,' she protested. 'We only do it in the afternoon.'

§

Sometimes it's hard to be a guy. We can surf easily between Chomsky's home page, Teen Anal, Theravada Buddhism and the cheat-code for *Grand Theft Auto* with scarcely a hiccup of bad conscience; the Net has externalised (and so part-socialised and normalised) a mental routine that hitherto had kept itself hidden, as we naturally assumed such ugly, unmodulated key-changes would be read as a sign of our moral degeneracy. Only an idiot would say this is a good thing, however; society is woven together by the collective denial of our nature. The leap from savannah to settlement to city was much harder for us, as our mind- and skill-sets were far less easily transferable. Had women not adapted so perfectly in a few million years, we would have cheerfully, and properly, taken another two billion over it.

§

Everything affirms the true faith. God's indifference is as much proof of His power as His intervention. The patent uselessness of prayer is joyfully understood as the corollary of His omnipotence – by which the believer understands His arrogation of *all* the power, their own tiny allotment included.

§

Yes I *know* Marcus Aurelius or Vauvenargues or Chesterton has already said this, and far more elegantly; but let's face it, you weren't listening then either.

§

R. enters the room in a wheelchair, barely able to form a sentence, and still the light in his eyes is undimmed. I find it hard to admire such *relentless* optimism: no doubt he would describe his glass as one-tenth full.

§

Anthony Burgess, reviewing a new edition of the *OED*, tested it by looking up his favourite *rechercherie*. He was pleased to find one particularly unusual word – but then saw that its single citation was given by Anthony Burgess. Did that supply a proof of the book's authority? Yes, if someone else looks up the word; no, if you are Anthony Burgess. Truth can be validated right up to its own front door, but no further, just as no god can confirm his own existence.

§

The badge of the intellectually insecure is their championing of the perfectly incomprehensible, their masterly interpretations of which can never be discredited.

§

The speed of light is only the defining *conceit* of this place. Other universes will have fallen apart in their own fashion.

§

Heavens, he really *did* think he had given my book a good review . . . In a year's time, he said (assuming, rather wonderfully, that I would file it away safely) – I would see that it was really full of praise. He had forgotten, of course, that his tortuous critique had appeared in a *newspaper*, and that its greatest design on posterity lay under a carpet. But of course he had imagined himself incapable of such a low act as mere *journalism*.

§

A stranger cycles past me in the street, then yells out at me, for no discernible reason – *You useless bastard!* My immediate response is *how does he know?*

§

I had badly miscalculated: when I kicked out God, he huffily took Satan with him, whereupon went my last excuse.

§

You are wrong about T.'s innocence being evidence of his 'good heart'; the fact that a washing machine or a toaster has no unconscious motive doesn't make it a saint.

§

I am sent a bundle of reviews and cuttings. I can now confirm that I have a small reputation as an intelligent and wise man; I also have another as an idiot and a fool. I have a small reputation as a man capable of courtesy and discretion; I have another as a graceless and loud-mouthed buffoon. I have a small reputation as a fine and original poet; I have another as an inept and derivative one. Accounting them all, they add up, precisely, to *nothing*.

§

First night of the flu last night. I dreamt, for what seemed like years, that I was a stand-up comedian, condemned forever to a disastrous routine of failed recognition humour: *... You know every time you count from one to ten, there's always one number over? You know when you go to the Gents, and there's always that smell of creosote in the first cubicle? You know how after you come and you're bleeding from your eyes and all these fucking* dwarves *show up?* It was no more than the amplification of my waking paranoia: that I have nothing to trade, that I am anecdotally bankrupt.

§

I wrote a blank poem once, which was immediately denounced as passé and unoriginal. But the basilisks that guard the original poems all hiss *cliché, cliché* . . . And sure enough, the gesture turned out to be not nearly as common as they had supposed. Indeed, a sad glance at my royalty statement tells me it is my most anthologised piece.

§

Went to see our new Hollywood Passion. Some kind of cultural watershed, surely: the point at which we finally succeeded in *exaggerating* Christ's agony.

§

The doors in the carpenter's house had been so beautifully hung they were impossible to open, having created a vacuum seal around their edges. He had to remove them all then replane their sides imperfectly, so his children could get to the bathroom again. This broke his heart. Our dreams so often exceed what the world is capable of expressing.

§

The beautiful can often only relax in the company of the ugly. This does not, alas, relax the ugly, but does lead to a great deal of bewildered sex between the two parties.

§

One spare and brilliant book every eleven years; then they change his meds and he cannot stop writing. Worse, he thinks he has discovered a sense of humour. For a man in the last fifth of his span, about as likely as discovering he had been black all his life.

§

Three days of email, it transpired, had been delayed for a whole month; and for that whole month I had been tormented by my new talent for obscure, violent and universal offence.

§

They awarded my Calvinist friend another prize, and he took to his bed immediately. He began to suspect a conspiracy.

§

After he had blessed my children, the Lama showed us to the door, still smiling hugely. Just before I pulled it to, I looked back and was shocked to see his expression changed utterly – bored, tired, cleaning his glasses. In my disappointment, I felt the sudden furnace-blast of my own ego. I'd once had a similar experience after an audience with a mortgage broker, and felt nothing but a satisfyingly rich contempt at his two-facedness; but the lesson was identical, and so too should have been my reaction.

§

Our human convention is that reputations can only properly be decided by posterity; though this has less to do with time than the mere addition of another couple of planets' worth of opinion, from which some common sense must inevitably prevail. But to be the size of Jupiter, and see those world-class charlatans, ass-lickers and nincompoops find their level *in their lifetime . . .*

§

So many of my moral crises turned out to be not my own but someone else's that I had been enthusiastically *hosting*. These proxy torments are more exhausting than any others, since one has to construct both the guilt *and* the sin.

§

I was always appalled when a former lover took a new one. I wanted a purdah of mourning, for the lot of them.

§

R. was so pleased with his review of my book, and could not see why I was not just as delighted. What offended me was his assumption that we publish these things and then sit around waiting for the response of him and his kind *to see whether or not they were any good*. We send these books out *believing* they're good, and would not do so otherwise. The good review doesn't fill us with joy; it only returns us to a state of equanimity. The bad drives us to despair. Thus, at the end of it all, we can never be in credit. Publication is, let us never forget, a synonym for *exposure*, a straightforward exercise in shame.

§

An aphorism quoted in the paper – and the italics have fallen off yet again, presumably on the instructions of the same teenage sub who thinks that a semicolon is a full stop in a state of weedy indecision. For the last time: in a form with no context, overstressing is a *necessity*.

§

God was only invented to protect the soul; the soul is just an erroneous back-formation from the ego; the ego is just an inwardly projected, spectral self-image which has arisen from the feedback loop of our individual consciousness, and that consciousness itself, only a tool possessed by a unit mammal which found itself in need of some half-decent predictive capability. In the name of which little skill we have immortalised ourselves, projected ourselves into an eternity on which we have not the slightest foothold.

§

My parents conceived me, the universe conceived of me.

§

I finally confessed to myself a vein of simple wickedness.
This saved me a lot of time and energy I would otherwise
have wasted in self-justification.

§

I am dismantled by a male critic, and spend the weekend
playing a violent video-game in invincible-god mode,
arming myself only with a dinner fork; by Monday I have
absolved him, and by Tuesday he is forgotten. I am dismantled by a female critic, and become hopelessly
aroused, soon wholly obsessed with this woman who has
taken such a specific *interest* in me . . .

§

Of my male friends, maybe three have survived middle age
with their hearing intact, and do not think almost continually and morbidly of themselves. (Well, maybe two;
one died rather than face that possibility.) Nearly all the
women have become less afraid. Even the childless seem to
know themselves to belong to a generative species. But
every man is a dead end, and he finds it out sooner or
later.

§

The memory of the symphony, painting, film or novel is
no more than that – a memory. But to remember a poem
is the poem; hence our making a fetish of its memorability.

§

The holy book is a disease of degree. The first stage is the declaration of the text as incontrovertibly brilliant: this is the first step towards the elision of the author. As the book begins to slip the moorings of its lowly human origin, soon the text will be shown to have merely *obtained*, its consonantal scratching found on some tablet or monolith – itself merely a copy of some timeless and distant incunabulum. Note that the *Tao* and the *Dhammapada* – two books that have become neither litanies of superstition, calls to war, nor lexicons of moral excuse – have both retained their authorship.

§

Foolishly, I buy a book on the strength of its cover quotes: several reviewers call it an 'instant classic'. It may well have been.

§

Heavens, it was a challenge, but I eventually found an insult he could not absorb. I suspect he was merely *full*.

§

People are their own blind-spots. All well-enough known, but it should be turned more often to our own advantage. For example: resubmit the work in the name of a rough anagram of the editor, and you will invariably find their opinion of it has dramatically improved.

§

A well-judged compliment briefly confers a cloak of invisibility on the one who pays it. While you receive one, hold on to your wallet.

§

After my ten-minute machine-gun raga guitar solo, my
father threw me, gently, out of his country-and-western
band. We are frogmarched from the genres by their
guardians; they know that anything beyond the smallest
mutations will destroy them. Postmodernism is really just a
club for the turfed-out, for all those unwelcome Lamarck-
ians, still bewildered at our failure to praise all the *leaps*
they were making . . .

§

Try as he might, he could not get his face out of the mirror; to his great exasperation, he always blocked his own
view. Of course deep down he knew that the transparen-
cies he sought were not in the mirror at all, but to look
anywhere else would by then have been inconceivable.

§

At enormous expense, he has turned the vast grounds of his country pile into a 'Garden of Cosmic Speculation', full of the most tasteless enormities: hills carved as double helices, hideous fractal patios, artificial lakes in the shape of Strange Attractors, equations sculpted in concrete . . . Some minor composers have been 'inspired', implausibly, to write works about it, and it is open to the public (here, the *priceless* detail) on just one day of the year. Behold, poor mortals, your Eden *today* . . . But the garden has long gone rotten in its knowledge, and come closing time we cast ourselves out again with inexpressible relief.

§

The ex-working classes can never quite believe themselves to be more than the sum of their good connections; too many of them assume that namedropping is one of the social graces.

§

He could never pay a compliment without bracing it on a slur; without it he would have been flung backwards on his arse, as from a cannon recoil.

§

As a journalist he was a disgrace to his profession, which is to say he was a credit to his profession.

§

She was a burning bush, a screaming silence, and we were all incinerated as we leant in to decipher the white noise of her.

§

Read *The Book of Disquiet* again. Scoured it for those brilliancies that are supposed to abound therein, but found nothing but a pretentious whiner of frankly average intelligence. More wisdom in any random episode of *The Simpsons*. Everyone loves the *idea* of Pessoa; but he's really one of that small class of authors best appreciated unread.

§

Terrifying, unthinkable – to realise that this universe only ever takes its form in the mind of one individual. No wonder we had to invent an all-seeing eye; the alternative was to place a near-infinite trust in one another. Without our gods to lift this responsibility, we would never have laid one stone on top of another, for fear all was phantasm.

§

Shocking to think that of all the million words I have typed into this machine it has not understood *one* of them. Yet I would not carelessly insult it.

§

The bare tree is still in the wind, as we are when we shed the leaves of our selfhood. Every thought slides through us like smoke through the branches.

§

M. is gaining a fine reputation for spotting great literary talent among the recently dead: they're barely cold before he's down at the mortuary, stitching the coat-tails to their blue arses. Having been stared over, through and past at one too many launch-parties, he knows better than to ever praise the living again.

§

V.'s every article berates the egocentrism and self-regarding nature of the 'poetry scene', its vicious infighting, nepotism, its lack of generosity . . . Like a man with a tannoy standing in the middle of a field no one ever bothers to cross, warning of the presence of a single sheep-turd.

§

After a wretched, overlong and convoluted guitar solo, full of badly executed quotes from Coltrane and Keith Jarrett, an older musician whispered in my ear: 'Never be afraid of what's easy on your instrument.' Indeed, what's easy is what is most characteristic; what is difficult is what is against its native grain and resonant possibility. Good general advice, and a superb retort to the *avantgardistas*.

§

The last thing I have written is always my favourite because I still host it; it is still me, is still in my body, in the wet red mill of my brain, and your insulting it can physically injure me. Say what you like about my first book, whose author is a complete stranger.

§

Poets dream within their imaginative elsewheres. In Scotland we live with very occasional illumination, so ours is actually a rather sunlit verse; by contrast, the Spanish poet is stalked by shadow.

§

Of the classes of metaphor, the prepositional is the most culturally insidious and hard to eradicate. There are underinterrogated consequences, for example, in thinking that we always write poems 'on' or 'about' a subject. In doing so we are often just extending our imaginative hegemony in another act of fatal misappropriation. We fall *in* love; so our lover feels entitled to assume that when our feelings undergo any complex change, we have simply fallen back out again. The Greeks thought of their future as behind them, and their past in front where they could see it; how much human misery has been caused by the dumb and hubristic inversion of that wholly sensible model?

§

Placing ourselves in complete chaos forces the creation of a centre. For those who have lost theirs, a good tactic of last resort.

§

Pedant at the guitar clinic: '. . . the available choice of *plectra* . . .' – both correct, *and* a stupid affectation; the word is possibly current amongst concert mandolinists, but beyond that queer milieu you will impress no one but the shade of Fowler. Best speech lies in its judicious concession to bad speech.

§

I suspect the real 'trick' – if indeed it is a trick – with women is: a) to simply love their company, and be unable to disguise it; and b) be confident enough either in yourself or your other arrangements *genuinely* not to care overmuch whether they will sleep with you or not. Feigned indifference is hopeless, and transparent. Desperation *stinks* to most women. But your visibly *not* hanging on the outcome of the evening is often a red rag to a bull.

§

Only the mad are safe from doubt. I am always bewildered by those who regard a revised opinion as a sign of weakness; it strikes me as a fine guarantee of the commentator's sanity.

§

It's monstrous to think of our parents having sex, because we then have to think of them conceiving *us* . . . Hard enough to live with the exile, without replaying the scene of the eviction.

§

Glamour is a sister of Hope. As soon as the guns fall silent and we're fed and warm again, little Glamour creeps out from under the stairs, with her filter-tips and kitten heels.

§

Good workmen blame their tools too; there's such a thing as bad tools. *Really* bad workmen utter no complaint, ask to be paid cash, and run.

§

A poem with one line wrong is like a Rubik's Cube with one square wrong: what it is precisely *not* is one move away from completion.

§

Never let the gesture drown the sign.

§

So many of the things we desire are now digitisable; as a result the whole idea of ownership will soon be eroded. At the time of writing, our download speeds are still slow enough to give us the illusion that *something* is being acquired; but if the transaction becomes instantaneous, that will disappear. At that point, the artefact – the book, the movie, the painting, the recording – will became wholly dereified. We would then see that there is *nothing to be gained*, since we could instantly inherit a greater amount of material than we could work through in several lifetimes; and then, that these things are better held in common store – the great libraries, music collections or movie databases accessed from our always-online, massive-bandwidth personal termini. Privilege of Access will then be valorised as possession now is, and we'll probably see the smooth transfer of our acquisitory fetish from one to the other. But the absence of *any* physical artefact or exchange will be significant: we may even see the idea of cultural wealth return to what our brains can hold, not our houses or our hard-drives.

§

My only decent students have all regarded poetry as their secret shame, an exercise in disgrace.

§

One of the interesting things about mid-life, he told me, is that there is a very short period where your sexual partners might be drawn from a thirty-year age range. Then one night, purely aesthetic considerations do for one end, and justified self-consciousness the other – the light stays off, or the vest stays on – and the bandwidth shrinks by twenty years again.

§

Our 'wonderful variety of regional accents' has been achieved by ensuring that half the population can't afford to travel more than ten miles from their birthplace. Nothing guarantees cultural diversity like geographic isolation. (The St Kildans developed an incomprehensible form of Gaelic consisting mostly of speech impediments. Should we *rejoice* in this fact?) For the most part, this diversity can only be enjoyed by those moneyed travellers who can register the differences, which almost defines them as a class of cultural abstainer. As a *cause*, then, diversity can only be championed by those who least embody it. Not that any of this is wrong; just that we should accept that most arguments to preserve it are wholly paternalistic.

§

My fear of flying has absolutely nothing to do with a fear of death, but on the contrary one of being *alive*, in all its precarious horror.

§

God's joke, maybe, but he should work on his timing. I always had the feeling the Big Bang was a little precipitate. Nothing seemed *ready*.

§

Your sincerity is neither here nor there. Writers sweat to write like lunatics, and painters sweat to paint like children. (By which I mean *talentless* children.) I know men who have spent thirty years learning how to sound like they're playing the piano with their backsides. If just one brave pair of buttocks had taken the stand beside them . . . As it was, they remained perennially oblivious to the shortcut, and thought their time well spent. I once sat through an hour of a man demonstrating his new technique for playing the saxophone: he sucked instead of blew. We punished him beautifully, however. We listened to him patiently; we gave him *every encouragement* . . .

§

The transcendental power of the dystopia. At the worst times in my life I have always sought to create them – socially, sexually, geographically – so that I might enact an *escape*, which might then grow into a more generalised tactic.

§

All arts have their bass solo – the sestina, the lino-cut, the one-woman play, those tours-de-force that we admire not because they survive their perverse form with any style or aplomb, but manage to do so at least without the total sur-render of dignity; and that we applaud wildly, out of sheer *relief* . . .

§

R. has taken an *age* to die. We had reckoned on a few weeks, followed by five or six months' decent grace – then the brutal reappraisal of his work we all feel long overdue. Our frustration is starting to show, though. Any more procrastination, and we'll dismantle him where he lies.

§

Each white page, another invitation to the mark of genius! Suckered into ruining it every time.

§

Always plant a quiet line that critics can damn you with: this proves they were always hunting for it.

§

How often as a child I entered that infinite realm; yet I brought back not a single word to assuage my adulthood.

§

Sense is the carrier-wave of truth. A tautology in all company but that of the Postmoderns, who it will one day strike with the force of revelation.

§

Writers can redeem a wasted day in two minutes; alas this knowledge leads them to waste their days like no one else.

§

A brilliant idea at 2 a.m., so fine and original I had no need to write it down. Gone forever by dawn, of course. Proof again, if I needed it, that I carry the abyss inside me.

§

No matter how ill-matched they are, any couple stupid enough to have sex with their eyes open are vulnerable to love.

§

He was starting a little poetry magazine, and asked me if I had any advice for a budding editor. The only thing I could think of was *open all the mail away from your face.*

§

Just occasionally, this little nation of stoics makes me weep with pride. 'Happiness', he declared, his beer-glass drenching his shoes, 'is for *poofs*.'

§

Valium and Black Label; *enjoy the flight*; the declared prospect of heavy turb over Malaga, and three hours in which to anticipate it . . . Why, then, when I so often profess nothing but contempt for this heavy existence, this rage of the flesh? Precisely that: I have fear of dying in the wrong element because it will not properly negotiate my release: *I cannot return my weight to the air*. I wish only to render to Caesar that which is Caesar's, and dread my life being derelict in its last transaction.

§

The bald ape has committed what is probably the universal *defining* error of the doomed intelligence: it has mistaken its dream for its element. Such carelessness will soon see it translated to the wrong one, where it will find itself irredeemably grounded, beached, drowned. If we're typical, no wonder the skies are silent.

§

Making a child is the opposite of killing someone. But there are still occasions when the former is the misdeed and the latter the kindness.

§

That exculpatory note, that letter that would come clean, explain everything . . . He spent so long drafting and redrafting it, he realised it would actually be an easier matter to maintain the lie and just outlive them all.

§

Such little memory as we recover from early childhood is really archaeology. In those seeds and potsherds we read the charmed domesticity of the ancient dead, moving through the day in their honeyed, eternal light.

§

The blessed lives we will not live: heaven is their promise, hell their abolition; but purgatory is their continual taunt, and its medium the living present.

§

My school-friend was incredulous: I had bought my father's old guitar with money from my Saturday job. Incomprehensible to the middle classes, of course, but the poor buy and sell from their parents and children, *to seal the money in.*

§

In our self-loathing we are most beguiled by those who are beguiled by themselves; they are our only real ambition.

§

What kind of life would I have led without my glamorous double, who took all my missed opportunities? A tolerable one, for a start.

§

I am only too quick to credit strangers with either enormous sophistication or enormous stupidity; I flip between complete deference and complete condescension, so violently that I think of myself as two different men.

§

What will keep me coming back here is not women, but guitars and libraries, the daydreams of which calm me so deeply, *resign* me so painlessly to this life – I could almost get to like it here.

§

Yet another refutation of rhyme from a *modernista*. Ah, how some people are assuaged when they can codify their failings, then transform them to a *choice* . . .

§

Astonishing, the number of mere acquaintances who immediately presume my confidence. If only they knew how hard my *closest friends* have had to work for it.

§

Personality is a mask we can't prise off, but no less a mask for that; only death removes it. When we feel it lift away from our suddenly weightless faces . . . we will experience our first real moment.

§

Putting up a couple of shelves badly can save you a lifetime of putting them up well.

§

I love Auden's snarl at an underwhelmed boyfriend: 'If you want romance, fuck a journalist.' Yet the poet's proud lack of romance is precisely their romantic delusion – and, as so much of their art is predicated on it, they are prevented from giving it its real name: a pathological insensitivity to the feelings of others.

§

In music production, we isolate a problematic frequency by sweeping the spectrum with a high-gain spike, until it reveals itself by wailing – and then *reduce* the gain at precisely that point. A man's diversions and hobbies denote those areas – his precise boredoms, his obsessions, his fears, his physical weaknesses – where he has, as it were, pulled himself down in the mix. A clever torturer might identify and attend to just those points of de-emphasis, reverse them, then turn them up until they scream.

§

True zealots are betrayed by their admiration for their enemies, and their hatred of those who differ from them by one degree.

§

The poorest are denied their nostalgias by their social immobility. Their primal territories are the ones they still inhabit. Their sweetest memories are all ungeographic.

§

His corpse was beyond such trifling repose as mere peace. He had *left time*, and I could not help but reflect on the elegance of the move. Even my slow walk from the funeral parlour to the Tube station felt like an epileptic fit.

§

I stopped writing when my behaviour became so extreme as to cease to be representative. If no one but you can verify the accuracy of your insight – it is, technically, barren.

§

Ah, the Yanks: every second poem a bloody manifesto.

§

Anything but the truth as our epitaphs. Mine would read
*His happiest hours were spent programming drums into a
midi sequencer.* T.'s: *Nowhere was he more fulfilled than in
those days he spent rearranging the copies of his own books
on the shelf, readying the room for the Great Visitor he knew
would never arrive.* L.: *His only serenity was in the silence
following one of his devastating insults.* B.: *Without dark
chocolate, her life would have been infinitely the poorer.*

§

'So what did you think of my piece about J.'s book? I thought it was very *reasonable*.' (J. is an author I publish.) 'What review?' I replied, honestly. He was incredulous: '*What* review . . . !' No: I assured him I was quite ignorant of it. Then he gave the name of a small magazine I had barely heard of. It seemed otiose to remind him that the occasion for our conversation was J.'s own funeral, which he had obviously marked down in his calendar as another *soirée*.

§

When I move from noun to verb I disappear from the world. To have only worked, slept, made love – and never once to have noticed yourself, to die still *unacquainted* . . .

§

The soul is accessible only by sympathetic resonance, like the horse's skull placed in the corner of the room by guitarists: the mind can't touch it, but the true symbol, image or word can set it moaning.

§

Between the ages of seven and twelve, I did nothing but study origami . . . and for what? Four years ago, in a Belgian bar, I folded Adolfo Cerceda's exquisite *Peacock* from a ten-euro bill for a beautiful girl from Kiev. I recall Robert Harbin's marginal comment on this model in *Secrets of Origami* – 'Now wait for the oohs and aahs' – which, being all I have ever desired from an audience, made the palms of my hands ache when I first read it. Anyway, the girl reacted appropriately, I guess; she widened her eyes, she made a little O of surprise; then she flattened the note out and bought two beers. I *still* don't get it. I can look forward to underwhelming my grandchildren on my deathbed.

§

Possession by demons is only an inconvenience when they are not fully assimilated.

§

I wouldn't sell my drafts for the earth. I wonder if I would ever have had a single decent review if they had known how I had cut these things from a block of raw error.

§

Speed up its evolution, and it becomes clear that the eye is not a receptive aperture but an exit wound, the catastrophic projectile fire of mind into the world.

§

The aphoristic form is closest to the appearance of honesty, and thus potentially the most subversive.

§

All I learnt was discretion.

§

My new book arrived, and I had no idea who had written it. Or at least I then understood *why* I had written it: to expel the last man. Forgive me this book; but as you can see, I could live with him no longer.

§

An exhibition of Dutch art: Rubens has everything leaning this way, or that way, with all the dynamic nuance of a Walt Disney. And then Vincent, who always understood that there are always at least three different winds in the sky, and that the hellish intricacy of their interaction is the reason we cannot hope to comprehend the motives or forces driving *anything*.

§

Those wholly estranged from themselves only have two real homes: the monastery or the stage.

§

On the clapped-out, bald-tyred council bus, hurtling
down the dual carriageway at 70 mph in the lashing rain.
All of us calm, reading, talking, absorbed, bored – but for
one terrified dog, yowling and yelping as if he is being
thrashed with a stick. The one animal amongst us still able
to respond *proportionately*, the only one still in possession
of his sanity.

§

When poets are asked their occupation – that is to say
what consumes their energies – they should answer, 'Not
writing.'

§

Consciousness can no more unmask its own nature than
the eye can see itself. It is contractually blind.

§